Computer Awareness

By

Parul Srivastava

(MCA)

Welcome to Computer Awareness by Parul.This book is useful to people who are giving entrance exams and competitions.It is also useful for novice beginners in computers.This book has been created especially for nurses undergoing BSc Nursing.

When going through the book you will learn all about Computers and MS Office.MS Office includes MS Word, MS Excel, MS Powerpoint and MS Access.All chapters are copyright to Parul Srivastava 2015.All Rights Reserved.No part may be reproduced,copied,modified,adapted without the prior written consent of the author.

I dedicate this book to my Parents....

Table of Contents:

COMPUTER FUNDAMENTALS

The word computer has come from a Latin word 'Computerae' that means to compute.

A computer is an electronic device which receives 'data' as input,processes it and produces result as output.

Computer in early stage

In olden days,we calculated using our fingers.Even today,we can use the same formula.Different methods were invented to do the calculation accurately and fast.The story of computer had started long ago.Since then it had undergone many stages.

Some early computers

Abacus was the earliest calculating device,invented in

China.It was invented mainly for counting.

Napier's Bones,a calculating device for multiplication,division,addition and subtraction was invented by John Napier.

Pascaline,a calculating device was invented by Blaise Pascal.Pascal is a numerical wheel calculator.

Difference Engine:Charles Babbage is the father of computer.He designed Difference Engine to calculate mathematical table.He then designed Analytical Engine which had many similarities to modern computer.

Calculator and Computer

Calculator

- There is only one part of calculator.

- Screen of calculator is very small.

- It works very slow and do simple calculation.

- It cannot do lots of work.

- There is only numeric key in calculator.

Computer

- Computer has basically four main parts as Keyboard,CPU,Mouse,Monitor.

- It has a big screen.

- It can do simple and complex sums.

- It can do lots of job as you can paint,read,draw with a very fast speed.

- The keyboard has number key,alphabet key and special key.

Computer-A Machine

Aeroplane is a machine which flys in the air and carries passengers to distant places.

Calculator is a machine which helps us to calculate.

Bus is also a machine which runs on road and carries passengers.Sewing machine is used to stitch clothes.

Telephone is also a machine which helps us to

communicate.

Similarly computer is also a machine.

Computer:An Intelligent Machine

A machine is a man made device which makes our work easier.Machines help us to work faster and correctly.

A refrigerator is a machine that keeps things cool.

Washing machine washes our clothes.

Mobile phone helps us to communicate with friends,parents.

TV shows cartoons,movies,news and other programs.

Motorcycle helps us in going to different places and enjoys riding.

AC helps to keep room cool.

Calculator helps in doing arithmetic operations like addition,subtraction,multiplication and division.

Likewise a computer is also a machine that works for you smartly.It works on electricity.It stores information and does calculation.

A computer is a smart machine because it works faster than us,it has memory like us and can store information.

It never commits mistakes.

It never gets tired.

It helps us playing games,surfing Internet,sending email.

Computer Generation and their Type

Classification of computer according to the technology used:

First Generation of Computers

The first electronic calculator MARK-I started the first generation.This machine was very slow but it could perform basic arithmetic   as well as more complex equations.

Characteristics of first generation computers:

- Used vacuum tubes.
- Had huge size.
- Large number of air conditioners were used.
- A single program was loaded.
- Very delicate and not reliable.

- Used magnetic drums for storage.

Second Generation of computers

The major development that had started the second generation of computers was the invention of transistor. Vacuum tubes were replaced by transistors in the computers of second generation.

Some characteristics of second generation computers were:

- Used transistors instead of vacuum tubes.
- Smaller in size and used less power.
- Had less heat production rate.
- Comparatively faster and reliable.
- Cheaper than first generation computers.
- Capable to handle a large amount of data.

Third Generation of Computers

Integrated Circuits were introduced in third

generation.

A single IC replaced a number of transistors because all the functions were performed by a single IC.

Some distinguishing features of computers of this generation were:

- Used Integrated Circuits(IC)
- Decreased in size and weight.
- Very reliable
- Cheaper than earlier computers.
- Could easily be replaced and maintained.

Fourth Generation of computers

The computers of this generation have been improved by reducing the size of IC.

Some characteristics of Fourth Generation computers were:

- Used microchip with a technique known as Very Large Scale Integration(VLSI).
- Reduced considerably in size.
- Low in cost,affordable to common man.
- Increased memory capacity.
- Worked with great speed.
- Developed network of computers.

Fifth Generation of Computers

Fifth generation of computers are based on artificial intelligence.With the use of artificial intelligence,computers can hold conversation with its human operators and can also learn from its own experience.

Types of Computers

- Micro Computers/PCs

- Mini Computers
- Mainframe Computers
- Super Computers

Micro/Personal Computer

Micro computers have brought revolution in computers because of their size and cost. All PCs come under the micro computers.

Common characteristics of micro computers are:

1. Cheap and easy to use.
2. Have limited input and output capacities.
3. Limited range of softwares can be used.
4. Have self contained units which can be moved easily.
5. Designed to be used by one person at a time.
6. Have CPU and a keyboard for input.
7. Hard disk and floppy disk drives are used to enter and store data and programs.
8. Monitor and printer are used to get the output.

Mini Computers

A. Mini computers are less efficient and store less data than mainframe computers.
B. Have limited range of peripherals.

C. Limited softwares are used.

D. Can be directly operated by the user.

WHAT IS COMPUTER?

A computer consists of many different parts. All these parts help us to do some work.

Some help us feed information into the computer others help us display the information and still other store the information for later use. We can, therefore, group the parts into input, output and storage device.

What is computer? Computer is a machine which runs on electricity and carries out our instructions.

Let us take example to understand the concept of input/output devices. When you have exams, you work hard. If you work hard, you get good marks. So, your working hard becomes an input. When you work hard, the output or result brings good marks.

PARTS OF COMPUTER

There are three main parts of computer:

1. **Keyboard**
2. **Central Processing Unit**
3. **Monitor**

KEYBOARD

Keyboard 100ks like a typewriter. It is made up of different types of Keys. These keys are small boxes on which some alphabets, numbers or signs are printed.

Alphabetical Keys: A, B, C,D,…….. to Z are English alphabets and the keys on which these alphabets are printed are called Alphabetical Keys. There are 26 alphabetical keys on the keyboards.

Numerical Keys: 0, 1, 2,…..to 9 are numbers and the keys on which these numbers are written are called Numerical Keys.

Special Keys : ?,!, #,%, & etc are called signs. These signs are present on the Numeric Keys.

CAPS LOCK KEY: This key is used when the entire sentence or word or a letter is to be typed in capitals.

Space Bar Key: The longest key on the keyboard is 'Space Bar Key'.Nothing is written on Space Bar key.

Enter Key: Enter key must be pressed after typing every command.

Shift Key: Shift key is present on both sides of the keyboard.Though both the keys do the same thing,they are provided for ease of working.

Delete Key:is used to remove errors from lines.

CENTRAL PROCESSING UNIT(CPU)

CPU is the brain of computer.As all thinking and calculation are done by brain,in the same manner all calculations are done inside the CPU.

MONITOR

Monitor is a display unit,it is also called as Visual Display Unit(VDU).It looks like a TV.
Whatever   we type from keyboard is displayed on monitor.

USES OF COMPUTER

1. School
2. Railways
3. Bank

4. Office
5. Home
6. Airport
7. Hospital

MAN AND COMPUTER

COMPUTER	MAN
Computer is always right.	Man would be sometime wrong.
Computer does not get tired.	Man gets tired.
Computer is fast.	Man is slower than computer.
Computer has no feeling.	Man has feeling.
Computer has no brain.It works on instruction.	Man has brain.
Computer can do only a few work.	Man can do all kinds of work.

Computer help Computer help everywhere-

1. Computer helps the doctor.With its help,the doctor can cure the disease very quickly.

2. Computer helps for booking ticket at railway

station and airport.

3. Computers are also used in offices,banks for calculation and for maintaining records.

4. Do you ever go to market?A computer helps in market.

5. We can write letters at the computer.

6. Computer helps in studies at school.

Uses of Computer

Computers are used at many places for performing many jobs.

One can write letters and send messages to one's friends and relatives through a computer.

One can also learn many new things with the help of the Internet on the computer.

A computer helps us in drawing pictures and painting on the computer.

One can listen to music and also watch movies on the computer.

We can play different games on the computer,like solitaire,minesweeper,Lionking.

It is also used for mathematical operations like addition,subtraction,multiplication and division

What is data?

Data has been derived from Latin word 'datum' which means facts.
Data is a collection of facts and figures which are unrelated and do not have meaning.

This data is converted into useful form by processing.

What is information?

Information is an organized collection of data.It is meaningful.

Computers and Us

Computers are helpful to us in many ways.A computer is sometimes better than us.

A computer has memory like us.

It works faster than us.

It never commits mistakes.

It never forgets.

It never gets tired.

It does not need food to get energy.

It never complains.

But in some ways,we human beings are better than computers.

We think on our own.

We do not work on electricity.

We have a brain.

We do not need orders to work.

Components of a Computer

A computer system has following components:

Input Unit

Example:
Keyboard,Mouse,Light Pen,Joystick.

Computer accepts data through an input unit.

Central Processing Unit(CPU)

CPU is the brain of computer.All processing work is done here.
It controls all the parts of computer system.

CPU is classified into following:

1)Arithmetic Logic Unit(ALU)

ALU performs all arithmetic and logic operations.It is made up of small locations called registers.

It has 2 parts:

A)*Arithmetic Section*: All complex arithmetic work is done here.

B)*Logic Section*: It performs logical operations as comparing,selecting and merging.

2)Control Unit(CU)

Control Unit gives command to transfer data from input devices to   memory and from memory to arithmetic logic unit.It transfers results   from memory to output unit.

Memory

There are 2 kinds of computer memory:

A)Temporary memory or primary memory

B)Permanent(secondary) memory

Following terms are related to computer memory:

1)RAM(Random Access Memory)

RAM is where all active programs and data are stored so that they are readily available to the CPU.

2)ROM(Read Only Memory)

Data stored on ROM cannot be changed.ROM is nonvolatile which means it does not get lost in the event of a power failure.

Output Unit

Example: Monitor,Speaker,Printer

Computer displays results on an output unit.

Software

Software is a set of instructions that directs the computer to process information.Computer software has various functions as controlling hardware,computations,communication with other software.

Software is classified into following:

A)*System Software*: coordinates the operation of various hardware components eg. DOS,Windows,Linux,UNIX.

B)*Application Software*: is a set of programs designed for specific   uses eg.MS Word,MS Excel,MS Powerpoint,MS Access.

C)*Utilities Software*:are those that are very often requested by many   applications.Eg.Antivirus software.

Hardware

Any part of computer that we can touch and feel is Hardware.
Eg. Monitor,printer,keyboard,mouse.

Data Structures

Bit:A bit is the most basic information unit.A single bit is a 1 or a 0,a   true or false,on or off.

Nibble:A nibble is aggregation of 4 bits.

Byte:A byte is aggregation of 8 bits.
                    1 Byte=8 bits

Kilobyte: A kilobyte is equal to 1024 bytes.
                    1 Kilobyte(KB)=1024 bytes

Megabyte:A megabyte is a computer storage unit of information
equal to 1024 kilobyte.
                    1 Megabyte(MB)=1024 kilobytes

Gigabyte:A gigabyte is unit of information equal to 1024 megabytes.
                    1 Gigabyte(GB)=1024 megabytes

Terabyte:A terabyte is a unit of information equal to 1024 gigabytes.

                    1 Terabyte(TB)=1024 gigabyte

MS WORD

The word processor is a software package which helps to enter and edit an entire document much faster than the usual manual way.MS Word is a window based application and is normally available in the program menu or in the desktop as an icon.

The menu bar provides access to the various word commands.The toolbar contains some useful buttons which help us to access some commands very quickly.

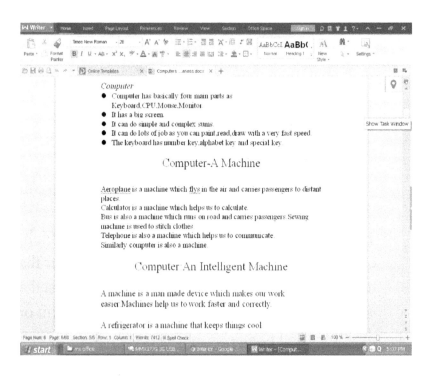

WPS Writer(MS Word)

The formatting toolbar helps to format the document.The Ruler is used to set the margin of the page and is also used to set tabs.

There are two options to work on a word document.Either you will work on the pre-existing file or you will create a new one.For this,

a)Click on File menu.

b)On the menu list that drops:

 click on Open menu,for pre existing file.

 Click on new menu,to create new file.

For saving a document,click on File menu and then Save.

Selecting text:

Steps:

- Bring cursor to left of the text.
- Hold shift key.
- Gradually keep on pressing the right arrow key of the keyboard.

Formatting

Now, when the text is selected, we can do various

formatting to the text.

Bring mouse pointer on B and then click it. Selected text becomes bold.

To bring it back to normal text, click it again.

To make the text italics, click I next to 'B'.

To underline text, click U button next to I.

To close all opened documents, click exit in the File menu.

Adding WordArt

- Select the text you want to convert into the WordArt.
- Click on Insert tab.
- Click on WordArt.A list of options appears.
- Click on the WordArt style you want to use.
- Type text.
- Click OK.

Creating a Table

Click in the document where you want to insert a table.

- Click on Insert.
- Click on Table.
- Enter rows and columns.
    Word adds table to the document.

Adding Page Number

- Click on Insert
- Click on Page Number.
- Click on location for page numbers.

Change Page Orientation

- Click on Page Layout.
- Click on Orientation.Orientation may be portrait or landscape.Click an option.

Word changes the orientation.

Inserting a Page Break

If you wish to start a new page at the same specific location in your document,you can insert a page break.

- Click in the document where you want to insert a page break.
- Click on insert tab.
- Cick on page break button.

Remove Page Break

- Click on Draft View button from the status bar to display the document in Draft View.
- A Page break line appears.
- Click on page break line and then press Delete key from the keyboard.

Changing Alignment of Text

Text can be aligned in different ways to enhance the appearance of document.By default,Word assigns the Left Align command.

- Select the text that you want to format.
- Click on Home tab.
- Click on one of the following buttons:
- Align Left to left align text.
- Center button to center text.
- Align Right to right align text.
- Justify button to justify text.

Changing the Line Spacing

- Select the text you want to use a different line spacing.
- Click on Home tab.
- Click on Line spacing to display the available line spacing options.
- Click on the line spacing option you want to use.

Changing the Color of Text

- Select text that you want to format.
- Click on Home tab.
- Click on down arrow of font color.
- Click on any color.

Changing the size of text

- Select the text you want to change to a different font.
- Click on Home tab.
- Click on down arrow of font size.
- Click on the size you want to use.

Count   words in a Document

When a work requires a specific number of words,you can use word count to count the number of words.

- The number of words in the document is the number across from word count.
- The number of words in the document appears on the status bar.

Set Line Spacing between paragraphs

The amount of space between paragraphs of text can be changed.

- Select the text that you want to format.
- Click on Home tab.
- Change   line spacing by line spacing option.

Creating a bullet or number list

Items in a list can be separated by beginning each item with a bullet or number.

Select the text to be formatted.
Click on Home tab.
Click on a list button.
Bullets button can be clicked to create a bulleted list.

Indenting a Paragraph

To make paragraphs in document,text can be indented.

- Select the paragraph needed to be indented.
- Click on Home tab.
- Click on increase indent to indent the left edge of paragraph.
- To decrease the indent,click on decrease indent.

Find and replace text

- Click at the beginning of document.
- Click on Home tab.
- Type the text you want to find.
- Type the text you want to use,in place of the text you typed.
- Click on Find.

Inserting Symbols

- Click on the location where you want a symbol to appear.
- Click on insert.
- Click on symbol.

Deleting   text in document

You can delete the text that is no longer needed.

- Select the text that you want to delete.
- Press the delete key from keyboard to remove the text.

Undo Feature

Click on open undo icon on quick access toolbar.

Word reverses the effects of the last change.

Copy and Paste

Select the text you want to copy.

- Click on Home tab.
- Click on copy.
- Click on the location where you want to place the text.
- Click on Paste.

The text will appear in the new location.

Open a saved document

- Click on File tab.
- Click on open button.

Recently opened documents appear on the File menu,and any of these documents can be clicked to open them.

Saving a document

- Click on File tab.
- Click on Save as button.

Spelling and Grammar mistakes

All the spelling and grammar errors in document can be found and corrected.

Click on Review tab.
Click on spelling and grammar button.

- There is an area which displays misspelled word or grammar error.
- There is also an area which displays suggestions for correcting error.

CREATE A LETTER FOR MAIL MERGE

- Open the Word document that you want to use as the letter.
- Click the Mailings tab.
- Click on Start Mail Merge.
- Click on Letters.
- Click on Select Recipients.
- The New Address List dialog box appears,displaying areas where information can be entered.
- Type the appropriate information for each person.
- To enter information for another person,click on New Entry.
- On finishing creating mailing list,click OK.
- Click on save button to save the file.

MS EXCEL

MS Excel is a powerful spreadsheet program that allows you to organize data,complete calculations,make decisions,graph data.

Excel allows you to organize data in rows and columns.These rows and columns collectively are called a *worksheet*.In electronic worksheet data is organized in same manner as manual worksheet.As like MS Word,spreadsheet has basic features to help create,edit and format worksheets.

Starting Excel

- Click start.
- Click All Programs.
- Click MS Office.
- Click MS Excel.

On opening Excel program,a blank workbook is displayed called *Book1*.

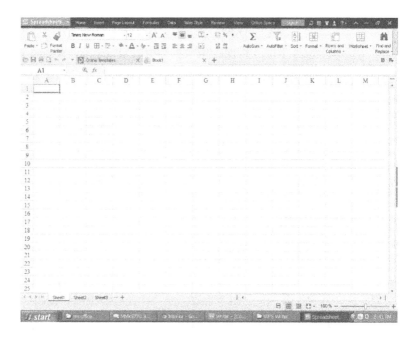

WPS Spreadsheet(MS Excel)

Title bar shows name of the displayed document.

File Tab help manage file information to save,open,print information for the document.

Quick Access Toolbar displays quick access buttons to save,undo and redo commands.

Program Window Controls buttons are used to minimize the program window,restore the window to full size or close the window.

The workbook contains sheets,called *worksheets*.A new workbook contains *three* worksheets.Each sheet has a name displayed on a sheet tab at the bottom of the workbook.

A *cell* is called the intersection of each column and row in a worksheet.A cell is the basic unit of a worksheet into which data is entered.

Each worksheet in a workbook has *16384 columns* and *1048576 rows*.

A cell is referred by its unique address or *cell reference*.To identify a cell,*specify column letter first,followed by the row number*,eg B8.

Formulas and Functions

Formulae are expressions which help you to calculate and analyse data in your worksheet.A formula in the worksheet always begins with an equal sign.

In maths,when you write a formula,you write out the values and the operators,followed by an equal sign(=).as 2+2=.

But in Excel,formulas begin with an equal sign(=),as =2+2.

Cell Referencing

Every cell in a worksheet has a unique address,also called a cell reference.

Cell Range

A group of related cells in a worksheet is called a range.Cell ranges are identified by their anchor points,upper left corner and lower right corner.The range reference includes both anchor points separated by a colon,eg A1:A3 includes A1,A2,A3.

Using Average,Max,Min Functions

If you want to calculate the average,highest,lowest sale of few persons in January,February,March from a range you can use functions like Average,Max,Min.

Excel,by default,includes formula called functions to help in computing the data.A function takes a value,performs an operation and returns a result to the cell,eg,=AVERAGE(G5:G14).

Creating a Chart

A chart can be created to compare data and view

patterns and trends easily.After creating a chart,chart tools on the ribbons can be used to fine tune the chart to display and explain the data.

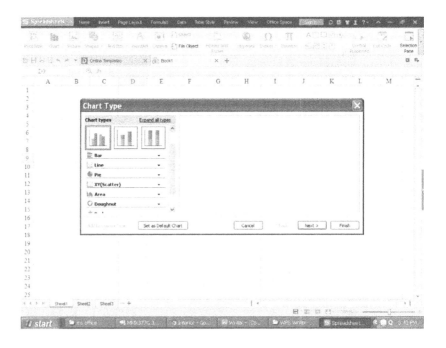

Chart in MS Excel

Select the range of data that you want on chart.
Click on Insert tab on the Ribbon.

Click on chart type from the Charts group.

Excel immediately creates a chart,places it on the worksheet.

Excel displays three chart tabs(Design,Layout,Format)for working with the chart.

MS POWER POINT

Powerpoint is the component of microsoft office.It combines text,clip art,drawing features and other objects to create self running or interactive display.

Powerpoint offers several advantages-

1.It navigates easily through the presentation.

2.It allows information from other sources to be available for presentation.

3.The computer uses the capability of its color to its full extent.

4.It utilizes multimedia effect.

5.Projection equipment is not required.

Getting started with MS Powerpoint:

- Click start.
- Click Programs.
- Click MS Powerpoint.
- Click Blank presentation.
- Enter title of your presentation.
- Enter subtitle.

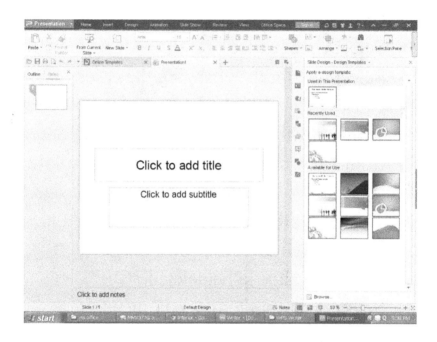

WPS Presentation(MS Powerpoint)

Insert Chart or Text:-

- Click insert.
- Click chart.

Or click pictures.

Or click on MS Word Table.

In word table enter the number of columns and number of rows.Type contents in word table.

- Changing the case of the text:
- Click format.
- Select change case
- Select text for the changing the case.
- Click OK.
  To display the slide,select slide sorter option from View menu.

Delete a slide

Select the slide to be deleted.
Select delete slide from edit menu.

Adding clip art pictures

- Click insert.
- Select clip art.
- Select the picture.
- Click on insert.

• Selected picture is inserted in slide.

Saving Presentation:

- From File menu select save as option.
- Save as dialog box is displayed.
- Click on Save button.

Various Effects in Slide Shows

Animations and Transition

Animations and transition are special sound and visual   effects that can   be added to text or other objects.

For making animations,go to animation tab,click custom animation and insert animation of your choice by clicking add effect.
Click Designs tab for different designs to insert in slide.

MS ACCESS

MS Access is a powerful database management system that functions in the windows environment and allows to create and process data in a database.Some of the key features are:

Data entry and update:Access provides easy mechanisms for adding,changing and deleting data,including the ability to make mass changes in a single operation.

Queries:Using Access,allows to ask complex questions concerning data in the database very easily and receive instant answers.

Forms:Access helps to produce attractive and useful forms for viewing and updating data.

Reports:Access contains a feature to create sophisticated reports easily for presenting data.

Database is a collection of data organized in a manner that allows access,retrieval and use of that data.Access allows to add,change and delete data in the database.

A database consists of a collection of tables in Access.The rows in the tables are called records.A field contains a specific piece of information within the record.

Starting Access

- Click on Start button.
- Click on All Programs.
- Click on MS Office.
- Click on MS Access.

Understanding Access Window

Title bar:It shows the name of the displayed database.

File tab:It displays file commands as New and Open.

Quick Access Toolbar:It displays quick access buttons to Save,Undo and Redo commands.

Status bar:displays information about the current object or view.

Create a New Table

- By entering data into a table,you can start a database.Tables consist of columns and rows that intersect to form cells for holding data.Each row is considered to be a record in a table.You can use columns to hold fields in a table.

- Click on create tab on the ribbon.
- Click on table button.
- Access opens a new table in datasheet view.
- Double-click the column header to create a field name.
- Type a name for the field.
- Press Enter key from keyboard.
- Click on next column.
- Select the data type for the field.Eg. select Text,if you want to add Name field.
- If you want to change the data type,click on the arrow button andame column.
- change the data type according to your need.
- After selecting the data type,its properties will be displayed in the lower pane.
- After selecting the data type,press the TAB key to move the insertion point to the description column.
- Press TAB key again to move to the Field Name column in the second row.
- Type the text in field name column.
- Press the TAB key to move to the Data Type column.
- The word 'Text' is currently displayed in that field.
- Press the TAB key to move the insertion point to Description column,if you want the data type as

text.

- Type the text for the description column.
- Repeat steps to make the remaining entries in the table to complete it.

Setting a Primary Key

A primary key is a key that differentiates the records in a file. The data stored in a key field contains data that is unique to a specific record. A student record, example, would use Roll number as a key field because it uniquely identifies each student.

In each new table that you create, you'll want to set one field as the primary key. Access uses this key to relate this table's records to those in another table.

Choose the field that you want to set as the primary key.

Click on the primary key button.

The field will be set as the primary key, indicating by a small key in the field of selector column. To remove it, select the primary key field and click on the primary key button again.

Save a Table

After creating a new table, it must be saved to make it a permanent part of the database.

Right click on the table's tab.

Click on Save.

Type a name for the table.

Click on OK.

The table remains open,and its new name appears on its tab.

Insert and Delete fields

New fields can be inserted and existing removed into a field list.A new row appears in the grid-above the one selected.

Steps-

Select the field where you want new field should appear above.

Click on design tab.

Click on insert rows.

A new row appears above the selected row.

Type a field name and choose a field type.

Select a field you want to delete.

Click on design tab.

Click on delete rows.

The row will be deleted,along with any data that the fields have.

Understanding Data Type

Each field has a data type that defines what you can store in it.Data entry is restricted to valid entries for the type you choose,which helps to prevent data entry errors.Example,you cannot enter letters in a field set to Number,and you must enter valid dates or times in a date/time field.

*Text:*This is a general purpose field containing any data.It has a limit of 255 characters and cannot be used for numeric calculation.

*Memo:*This has a limit of 63,999 characters;used for detailed,descriptive fields.

*Number:*This type stores numeric data that you can use in calculations.It can also hold symbols,as decimal points and commas.

*Date/Time:*This type only stores numbers representing valid dates and times.

*Currency:*Stores currency data that you can use in calculations.

Auto Number:stores a sequencial number for each record.

*Yes/No:*The value -1 represents Yes,and the value 0 represents No,but the field can be formatted to display values as True/False or Yes/No.

*OLE Object:*stores objects created in another application-as Word or Excel-that you can link to or fix in an Access table.

Hyperlink: You can link to websites,email addresses,files on your computer,files on any other location.

Attachment: You can attach data files.

Change Data Type

The data type of a field can be changed anytime to better represent data.Field types should be set before entering data into table,field type can be changed anytime.

Click on the down arrow to ope the Data Type list for the field.
Click on new type.
To save the changes to the table,click on save.
Click on yes to allow the deletion of records that violate the new field type's rules.
No can be clicked to abandon the change.

Rename a table

A table can be renamed at any time.Access

automatically updates all references to the table throughout the database. The table must be closed in order to rename it.

Right click on the table name in the navigation pane. A short cut menu appears.
Choose rename from the shortcut menu. The table name appears in edit mode.
Type the new name for the table and press enter key from the keyboard.
The new name appears on the table.
Click on the table name in the navigation pane.
Click on Home tab.
Click on delete button from record group.
A confirmation dialog box opens.
Click Yes.
The table will delete.

Adding Records to a table

The first step is to create a table by building the structure and saving the table. The second step is to add records to the table. The table must be open so that the records can be added to the table. The table displays in datasheet view. In datasheet view, the table is represented as a collection of rows and columns called a datasheet.

Double click on table in the customer:database window.

Type the customer id in the first customer id field.

Press the tab key to complete the entry for the customerid field.

Type the following entries by pressing the tab key after each one to complete the record.

After typing the last entry,press the tab key.

The insertion point comes to the customerid field in the second row.

Add the remaining records by following the same steps you used to add first record.

Click on save,to save the changes.

COMPUTER SECURITY

Now-a-days computers are becoming a reliable source to create,store and manage critical information.It is also crucial that users take measures to protect their computers and data from loss,damage,and misuse.For example,a company must ensure that information,such as credit records,employee and customer data and purchase information are secure and confidential.

Computer security risk is a term known for any event or action that could be harmful for a computer hardware,software,data information or processing capability.Some breaches to computer security are accidental while others are planned.Any illegal act involving a computer is generally referred to as a computer crime.The term cybercrime refers to online or internet-based illegal acts.

The following sections describes some of the more common computer security risks and safeguards,you can take to minimize or prevent their consequences.

Computer Viruses

Virus is a potentially damaging program in a computer,which negatively effects or infects your computer without your knowledge and alters the working of the computer.More specifically,a computer virus is a segment of program code from some outside source that implants itself in a computer.Once a virus is in your computer,your files and operating system may be damaged.

The increased use of networks,the internet and email has accelerated the spread of computer viruses.With these technologies,computer users easily can share files and any related viruses.Viruses are activated on your computer in three basic ways:

(1)Opening an infected file

(2)Running an infected program

(3)Booting the computer with an infected floppy disk in the disk drive.

The most common way of virus in a computer is through the attachment in an email.Before you open or execute any email attachment,you should ensure that the email message is from a trusted source.A trusted source is a company or person you believe will not send you a virus infected file knowingly. You should immediately delete any email received from an unknown source without opening or executing the attachment. Thus you can protect your computer against viruses if you follow the precautionary measures.

Viruses in computer are not generated accidentally but are programmed intentionally by a programmer known as a virus author. Some virus authors find writing viruses a challenge. Others write them to cause destruction. Writing a virus program usually requires significant programming skills. Some viruses are harmless ranksthat simply freeze a computer temporarily or display sounds or messages. The music bug virus,example,instructs the computer to play a few chords of music. Other viruses destroy or corrupt data stored on the hard disk of the infected computer. If your computer acts differently from usual,it may be infected with a virus.

Today,viruses pose as serious threat to the safety of a computer. Currently,more than million known virus programs exist with an estimated 6 new virus programs discovered each day.

Though there are numerous variations,3 main virus types known to exist are,boot sector,file and macro.

A boot sector virus also known as a system virus,executes

when a computer boots up because it resides in the boot sector of a floppy disk or the master boot record of a hard disk. When you leave a floppy disk in the floppy disk drive and boot up the computer, the computer attempts to execute the boot sector on the disk in drive A. The hard disk of a computer can be infected by any virus on the floppy disk's boot sector even if the disk is not the boot disk.

INTERNET

Internet also called net,is an electronic communication device.It is one of the largest networks that links millions of computers all over the world.This network can be accessed via communication devices and media such as modems,cables,telephone lines and satellites.

Some of the things one can do on the internet are communicate with others around the world,banking,investing,shopping,download,listen to music,watch movies,take a course,access educational material,access sources of entertainment and leisure as online games,magazines and vacation planning guides,exchange files,share and edit documents,provide information,photographs,audio clips,video clips.

Computers connected to the internet work together to transfer data and information around the world using servers and clients.The computer which is responsible for the management of the resources i.e. programs and data,on a network by providing a centralized storage area is called *server*.

The computer which has an access to the contents of the storage area on the server is called a *client*.

Equipment needed for internet

1. Computer
2. Modem
3. Telephone line
4. Speaker
5. ISP(Internet Service Provider)-bsnl,tata indicom,mts etc.

Website:A website is a collection of web pages maintained by a college,university,company,organization or individual.

*Webpage:*is an electronic document written in a presentable manner.A web page can contain text,graphics,sound and video,as well as links to other documents.

Searching Information on the web:

*Search by keyword:*To find web page of interest,you

can type a word into a search tool.The search tool will display a list of web pages containing the word you specified.Some search tools allow you to enter a complete question while searching for web pages.

Search using google:.

Google indexes thousands of web pages so that users can search for the information they desire,through the use of keywords.

Windows And MS DOS

Files and Folders in Windows

Windows helps to store files and folders.My Computer,My Picture and My Music are the three main folders in which Windows saves files by default.

Files:A collection of data or information that has a name is called the filename.There are various types of files:document files,text files,program files,directory files

Folder: Just like a file cabinet in the school,the computer also stores many files.Instead of dumping every file in hard drive,they can be arranged in folders.Some folders contain additional folders called subfolders.Computers can turn into centre of dump files and there will be difficulty in tracing out required file.

Rename a File

To better describe the contents of the file in a better way,rename a file.Renaming a file can help in locating the file quickly in future.

Restore a deleted file

The recycle bin stores all the files deleted.If any file has been deleted by mistake,it can be restored to its original location by the restore option.

Empty Recycle Bin

To create more space on the computer,recycle bin can be emptied.

When recycle bin is emptied,files are permanently removed from the computer and cannot be restored.

Backup Files

Backup of important files is made.This is useful when system causes to lose one or more files,they can be restored from backup.

DOS
(Disk Operating System)

DOS is not case sensitive ie DIR and dir are same.

While typing a command,if "Bad command or file name" message comes,it means DOS did not find any file name matching the request.So correct it and enter it again.

The file names are restricted to 8 characters only.

It does not support spaces in file name.

DOS commands :

cd..   Means change directory

cd D: means change directory to D

md xx   means make directory xx

dir D:|more means directory D page by page

C:\>copy con letter.txt

To,

The Principal,

            Kindly give me leave on 30 January,2015.

                        Thanking You,

                            YY

Ctrl Z

This commands means making a file letter.txt

Ctrl Z means saving file

To display letter.txt

C:\>Type letter.txt

C:\>Type letter.txt|more for viewing letter page by page

C:\>mkdir xx means make directory xx

C:\>rd xx means remove directory xx

C:\> dir|sort means sort directory

C:\>Ren letter.txt gita.txt means rename letter.txt to gita.txt

Other commands :

C:\>Date   is command for getting current date

C:\>Time   is command for getting current time

C:\>Ver   is command for getting version

Exercise 1

1. The first generation of computers were based on

A. Transistors
B. ICs
C. Valves
D. Conductors

Ans C

2. All computer processing is done in

A. RAM
B. Keyboard
C. Monitor
D. CPU

Ans D

3. The second generation computers used

A. Transistors
B. Chips
C. ICs
D. Valves

Ans A

4.Who is the father of Computer?

A. Newton
B. Lewinsky
C. Charles Babbage
D. Ted Hoff

Ans C

5.Fulform of RAM is

A. Read Only Memory
B. Random Access Memory
C. Ready Usable Memory
D. Random Added Memory

Ans B

6.Output can be obtained on

A. Keyboard
B. Monitor
C. Joystick
D. Mouse

Ans B

7.Debugging tools debug errors in

A. Programs
B. Keyboard
C. Printer
D. Mouse

Ans A

8.It is a collection of facts and figures

A. Information
B. Programs
C. Mouse
D. Data

Ans D

9.Printed copy is also called

A. Hard copy
B. Blank copy
C. Read/write copy
D. Soft copy

Ans A.

10.Main types of software are

A. New
B. Open
C. Application
D. Raw

Ans C

Exercise 2

1.The shortcut key for copy is

    A.   Ctrl + X
    B.   Ctrl + Y
    C.   Ctrl + C
    D.   Ctrl + S

    Ans C

2.Shortcut key of paste is

Ctrl + V
Ctrl + A
Ctrl + S
Ctrl + Y

Ans A

3.What is the extension of Word document?

    A.   .ext
    B.   .ppt
    C.   .av
    D.   .docx

Ans D

4.The name of the opening document in MS Word is

A. Document 1
B. Doc 2
C. Unnamed
D. New

Ans A

5.Word wrap is

A. Distance between lines.
B. Automatic placement of a word on next line
C. Attaching data
D. None of these

Ans B

Exercise 3

1.Group of worksheet is called

A.   Document
B.   Placeholder
C.   Book
D.   Work Book

Ans D

2.Data that is pictorially represented in worksheet is called

A.   Graph
B.   Chart
C.   Both a and b
D.   None of these

 Ans C

3.The number of rows in MS Excel is

A.   65,536
B.   65000
C.   60,000
D.   58000

Ans A

4.Number of columns in MS Excel is

A. 300
B. 500
C. 256
D. 250

Ans C

5.The extension of MS Excel file is

A. .ppt
B. .doc
C. .kbp
D. .xls

Ans D

6.In Excel all formula start with

A. +
B. =
C. -
D. @

Ans B

7.Anything that is typed in a worksheet appears

A. In formula bar only
B. In active cell only
C. In both active cell and formula bar
D. None of these

Ans C

8.Intersection of a row and a column in excel is called

A. cell
B. Block
C. Group
D. Point

Ans A

Below are Previous Year solved question papers of College of Nursing,Central Command,Lucknow.

BSc Ist Year Nursing

Prefinal Exam,2015

Introduction to Computers

MM:50

Choose the correct option.Write the option a,b,c or d in front of the answer number and the option.Example: 1.b)cell

1.Landscape is?

a.A font style

b.Paper size

c.Page Layout

d.Page Orientation

2.Which shortcut will we use to make text italic?

a.Ctrl+U

b.Ctrl+T

c.Ctrl+I

d.Ctrl+P

3.What is the use of "All Caps" feature in MS Word?

a.It changes all selected text into Capital letter.

b.It adds captions for selected image.

c.It shows all the image captions.

d.None of the above.

4.Which   is   not   a   font   style?

a.Bold

b.Superscript

c.Italic

d.Regular

5.Which of these toolbars allows changing of Fonts & their sizes?

a.Standard

b.Formatting

c.Options

d.None of the above.

6.Which is the default font size of a new Word document based on Normal Template?

a.8 pt

b.10 pt

c.12 pt

d.14 pt

7.Which is correct extension of Word file?

a).xls

b).doc

c).ppt

d).dcw

8.In Excel,if you press....,the cell accepts your typing as its contents.

a.Enter

b.Ctrl+Enter

c.TAB

d.Insert

9.You can use the formula in Excel to.

a.format cells containing numbers.

b.create & edit formulas containing functions.

c.enter assumptions data.

d.copy a range of cells.

10.Excel   is   a

a.Database program

b.Word Processor

c.A spreadsheet

d.None of these

11.To preview custom animation in Power Point,we should.

a.double click motion path

b.click show effect button

c.Click play button

d.None of these

12.Which of the following will not advance the slides in a slide show view?

a.Mouse button

b.Enter key

c.Space bar

d.ESC key

13.Give full form of SQL.

Answers

1d,2c,3a,4b,5b,6c,7b,8a,9b,10c,11c,12d

13.SQL:Structured Query Language

BSc Ist Year Nursing

Introduction to Computers(Theory)

Final Exam,2015

MM:50

Choose correct option.Each question is of 2 marks.

1)CD stands for

a)Compact Disk

b)Computer Disk

c)Connector DJ

d)None of the above

2)OMR stands for

a)Optical Mark Reader

b)Optical Mark Reading

c)Optical Mark Radar

d)None of these

3)How do you magnify your document?

a)View,Zoom

b)Format,Font

c)Tools,Option

d)New,Edit

4)What is the short key for CUT

a)Ctrl+C

b)Ctrl+M

c)Ctrl+N

d)Ctrl+X

5)Find a right email

a)shweta@india.com

b)shwetaindia

c)satyam+com

d)None of these

6) www stands for

a)World Wide Websites

b)World Wide Web

c)Word Wide Webs

d)None of these

7)Who is the father of Computer?

a)Shweta Tripathi

b)Tim Band Lee

c)Charles Babbage

d)Rudyard Kipling

8) KB stands for

a)Kaleidoscope

b)KiteBuy

c)Kilobig

d)KiloByte

9)What is used before formula in MS Excel?

a)Plus sign

b)Equal to sign

c)Minus sign

d)Multiply sign

10)Median is a

a)Language

b)Game

c)Statistical Function

d)None of these

11) CPU is the _____ of computer

a)Eye

b)Nose

c)Ear

d)Brain

12)Toolbar which changes fonts and their sizes is

a)Options

b)Zoom

c)Operator

d)Formatting

13)Shortcut key for italic is

a)Ctrl+B

b)Ctrl+C

c)Ctrl+I

d)Ctrl+M

14)Correct extension of Word file is

a) .abc

b) .doc

c) .div

d) .ma

15) Excel is a

a)Database

b)Word Processor

c)Spreadsheet

d)None of these

16) In Excel,intersection of row and column is called

a)Row

b)Cell

c)Column

d)None of these

17) Internet is an example of

a)Connectivity

b)Land

c)Earth

d)Animals

18)Read Only Memory is full form of

a)ROM

b)RAM

c)SAM

d)None of these

19)Keyboard is a

a)Output Device

b)Memory

c)Blog

d)Input Device

20)CapsLock prints

a)Capital Letters

b)Small Letters

c)Designs

d)None of these

21)Numeric keypad has

a)Alphabets

b)Photos

c)Numbers

d)None of these

22)To delete characters, press

a)Ctrl+A

b)Delete

c)Ctrl+9

d)None of these

23)Monitor is a

a)Hardware

b)Software

c)Book

d)None of these

24)Which is a sound file

a)LOG file

b)DAT file

c)DRV file

d)WAV file

25)All slides can be seen at once by

a)Kaleidoscope

b)Slide show

c)Mike

d)None of these

Answers to above Questions-

1a,2a,3a,4d,5a,6b,7c,8d,9b,10c,11d,12d,13c,14b,15c,16b,1
7a,18a,19d,20a,21c,22b,23a,24d,25b

Thank You

www.ingramcontent.com/pod-product-compliance
Lightning Source LLC
Chambersburg PA
CBHW071302050326
40690CB00011B/2503